T0151881

The Handbook of Palmistry

By

Rosa Baughan

WITH ILLUSTRATIVE PLATES

Plexus, London

PALMISTRY GUIDE BY CHEIRO THE PALMIST

Ruens & Venus
Mensalis
Mensalis
Epatica
Martis
Linea of Life
Vitae or
Restricta

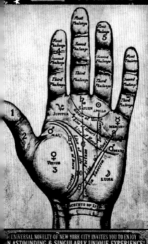

First Phalange
Second Phalange
Third Phalange

Jupiter   Saturn   Apollo   Mercury
Mars
Venus
Luna

Lenormand-Museum de MADAME LE NORMANDS
GIPSY FORTUNE TELLING CARD GAME
PUBLISHED BY WEHMAN BROS NEW YORK

AMERICAN PHRENOLOGICAL JO.
KNOW THYSELF
HOME TRUTHS FOR HOME CONSUMPTION.
1848.
VOL. X.   MARCH.   NO. 3.
O. S. FOWLER, EDITOR.
PHRENOLOGY, PHYSIOLOGY, PHYSIOGNOMY, MAGNETISM
NEW YORK:
FOWLERS & WELLS.

UNIVERSAL NOVELTY OF NEW YORK CITY INVITES YOU TO ENJOY AN ASTOUNDING & SINGULARLY UNIQUE EXPERIENCE!
!One Day Only!
THE MECHANICAL MYSTICAL ORACLE
ZANTHOR

KNOWS ALL, SEES ALL & TELLS ALL.
The ultimate form of automated divination with a direct link to the
Spiritual Plane AND **SUPERNATURAL REGIONS BEYOND**

Curious patrons of all ages are invited into Zanthor's sanctum for a FREE demonstration of his precognitive power to foretell the fate of those who dare to inquire! This consultation is ABSOLUTELY FREE OF CHARGE with NO purchase obligation or ANY contract of investment

PALMISTRY

ABCDEFGHIJKLMNOP
YES   NO
GOODBYE

MISS ROSA BAUGHAN'S WORKS.

PUBLISHED BY GEORGE REDWAY.

Price One Shilling.] *Fourth Edition, newly revised and enlarged, with Illustrative Plates.*

The Handbook of Palmistry.

"It possesses a certain literary interest, for Miss Baughan shows the connection between ...

"Miss Rosa Baughan, for many years known as one of the most expert proficients in ... on the subject."—SUSSEX DAILY NEWS.

"People who wish to ... reading character from the marks of the hand," says the DAILY NEWS, in an article devoted to the discussion of this topic, "will be interested in a handbook of the subject by Miss Baughan, published by Mr. Redway."

GEORGE REDWAY, YORK STREET, COVENT GARDEN.

Price One Shilling.] The

Handbook of Physiognomy.

"The merit of her book consists in the admirable clearness of her descriptions of faces. So vivid is the impression produced by them that she is able to dispense with illustrations, the reader using the faces of his acquaintances for that purpose. The classification, too, is good, although the astrological headings may be regarded by the profane as fanciful. Physiognomy may now be scientifically studied by means of composite photography."—PALL MALL GAZETTE.

GEORGE REDWAY, YORK STREET, COVENT GARDEN.

Price One Shilling.] *With Illustrative Plates.*

Chirognomancy;

Or, Indications of Temperament and Aptitudes Manifested by the Form and Texture of the Thumb and Fingers.

"Miss Baughan has already established her fame as a writer upon occult subjects, and what she has to say is so very clear and so easily verified that it comes with the weight of authority."—LADY'S PICTORIAL.

"Ingenious and not uninteresting."—THE QUEEN.

GEORGE REDWAY, YORK STREET, COVENT GARDEN.

'There are more things in Heaven and Earth
Than are dreamt of in your philosophy, Horatio.'
- William Shakespeare, *Hamlet*

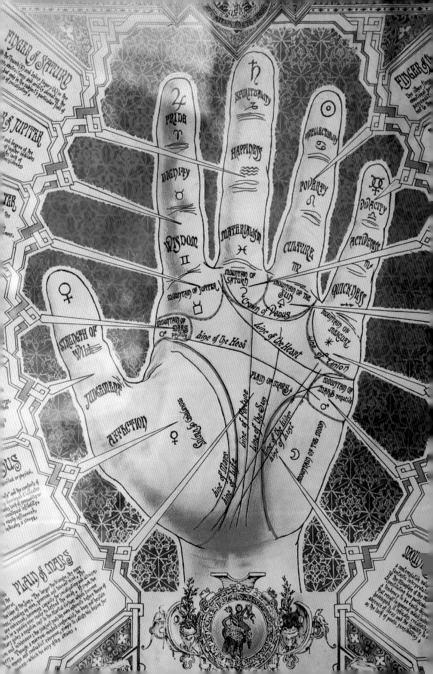

Contents.

Preface.

IN these days, when Realism over-rides the Ideal, it seems almost absurd to offer to the reading public even so small a *brochure* as mine on the old-world subject of Palmistry; but a superstition (if you will) which has attracted the serious attention of Aristotle and many other ancient writers, and among the modern, of Herder, Balzac, Desbarrolles, and a host of others, is at any rate worth considering.

Whilst at Paris, some years ago, I was shown by an intelligent Frenchman (who like myself confessed to be *almost* a believer in Palmistry) some very interesting drawings of the hands of Victor Hugo, Dumas, Lamartine, and other French celebrities; and, in all these drawings, the development of the lines and mounts showed exactly the qualities which we knew these men possessed; for instance, in Victor Hugo's hand we noticed that Jupiter and Venus were so prominent as almost to overpower the development

Empress Joséphine of France waits to hear her fortune, as read by palmist Le Normand in the Château de Malmaison.

of the rest of the palm. Jupiter (as will be seen) gives power, pride, imagination of the fervid order, and immense self-assertion; Venus, tenderness and passion. Are not these qualities shown in 'Notre Dame de Paris,' 'Les Misérables,' and, indeed, in all this author's works?

In the hand of Dumas, the Line of Head (which denotes intellect) is long and well developed, and descends, with vehemence, towards the Mount of the Moon, which is salient; which combination indicates, according to Palmistry, the almost Eastern imagination which produced 'Monte Cristo;' indeed, imagination would occupy the whole of the left hand, did not the Mount of Venus (passion) rise to meet it—there is no *want* of passion in Dumas' writing. In the right hand the Mount of Mars is very salient, which accounts for the action, energy, and spirited movement of all Dumas' historical works.

In Lamartine's hand we noticed the same long Line of Head, but not drooping so much to the Mountain of the Moon; but the Mount of Mercury was largely developed, and accounted for the eloquence of the language in his writings, whilst the Line of Heart, extending all across the palm and enriched by branches, explained the exquisite tenderness of his verse.

Other drawings, too, of the hands of well-known artists, seemed equally happy in bearing out the axioms of Palmistry, and, as I closed my examination of them, I could not help echoing my French friend's words: 'C'est, au moins, très curieux.'

R. B.

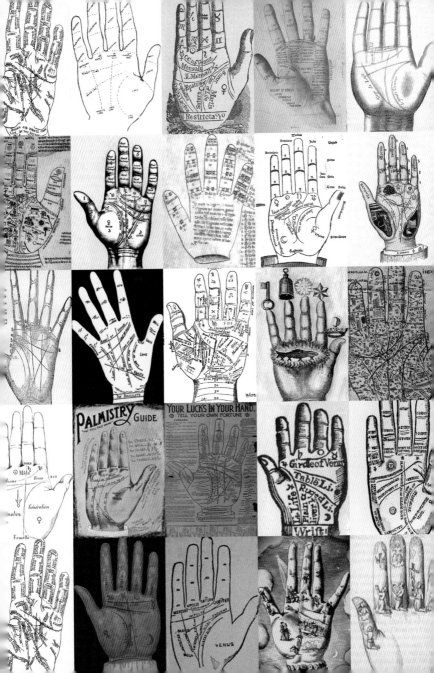

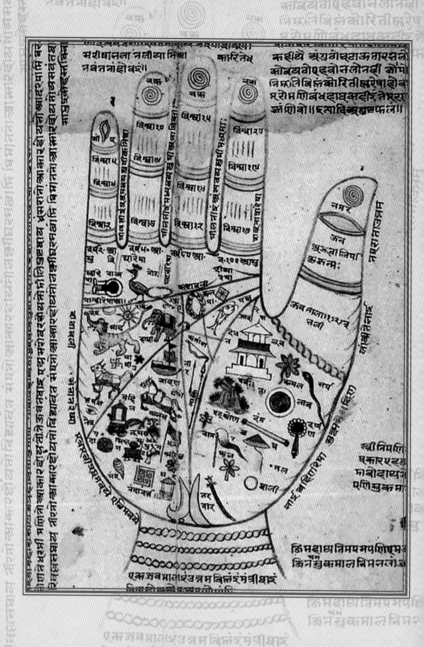

Chapter I.

The Doctrines of the Kabbala.

CHIROMANCY, or, as it is more generally called, Palmistry, is a science of great antiquity, as it is based on the doctrines of the Kabbala—the origin of which is lost in the night of ages. Whether it took its rise first in Chaldea, India, or Egypt is uncertain; but its doctrines were known to all these nations, and it is probable that such of them, as were afterwards introduced into Greece by Pythagoras, were acquired by him in his intercourse with the ancient Magi, during his travels in the East, which was, at that period, the region of all intellectual light. In the earliest ages, almost all the inhabitants of the earth led a pastoral life—were, in fact, merely shepherds; but amongst these shepherds, there naturally arose, from time to time, men of superior intelligence, whose imaginations (purified and strengthened by solitude and the constant communion with nature which grew out of that solitude) led them to the study of those

The oldest known manuscript of its kind, this 'smalle treatise
of palmestrie' is believed to date from 1440 or earlier.

distant worlds, which they saw night after night, appear and disappear in the cloudless vault of the heavens above them.

Of purer lives, more impressionable than we moderns, they were naturally more open to the influences of nature; and all their thoughts being given to the study of the mysteries by which they felt themselves surrounded, the magnetic power in man was revealed to them. This power they (the Kabbalists, or believers in the ancient Kabbala, some of the doctrines of which we shall explain farther on) designated by the various names of 'Inri,' 'Serpent,' and 'Lucifer,' and attributed to the result of astral influences exerted by the planet or planets dominant at the moment of the conception, as well as that of the birth, of the individual exerting it; this astral influence was, in fact, that latent power—that still almost unknown agent—which we moderns recognise under the names of electricity and animal magnetism.

The planets which the ancients supposed to have this power of influence were seven in number: Jupiter, Saturn, the Sun, Mercury, Mars, Venus, and the Moon. It may be objected that science has long since revealed to us many more planets than the seven known to the ancients, but (taking upon ourselves the Kabbalist's cause to defend) we would observe that Mercury, Venus, Mars, Jupiter, and Saturn are still the most important planets; Uranus would (according to Kabbalistic notions), from its immense distance, lose its influence upon us; and as to the other planets, Vesta, Juno, Ceres, and Pallas, their influences—small as they are—might be supposed to be annihilated by that of the larger celestial bodies of the seven planets recognised in the Ancient Kabbala. The Moon, though so small, might easily be supposed to have on us a

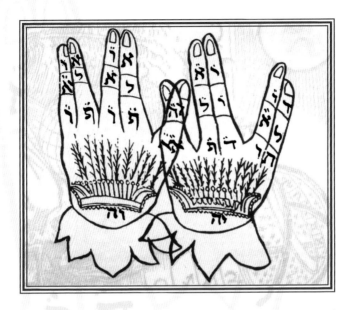

A Kabbalistic sketch showing the mystic connection between letters, numbers and the hand.

more subtle influence in consequence of its extreme nearness to us; we see that influence on the tides, and in other physical matters, whilst of the Sun's influence on us and the whole creation, there can, of course, be no question.

We shall presently show how the ancients recognised the different signs of the various influences of the seven planets on the hand; the lines of which were produced, they believed, by the astral fluid emanating from these planets. They held that each of these seven planets was in the ascendant once during the space of the twenty-four hours forming the day and night; thus, if a person were born under the junction of two or more planets, the marks in his hand would be found to partake of the signs, by them, attributed to the influence of *each* of these planets, but according to which was *most* in the ascendant, so would the signs be found to exist; for, although there would always be the sign of the planet dominant, it rarely if ever happened that one planet solely influenced the birth; in this way they accounted for the endless varieties, physical and mental, of human nature. Before, however, entering more fully upon the ground of Chiromancy, as it was understood by the ancients, it may be as well to give our readers a short account of some of the doctrines of the Kabbala, from which Chiromancy or Palmistry took its rise.

The 'Holy Kabbala,' as it was called by the Magi, must not be confounded with what is called 'The Black Art;' it is, on the contrary, the quintessence of reason and morality, as they were understood by the ancients—that traditional science of the secrets of nature which, from age to age, is borne towards us as the wave is borne by the tide to the shore; but it has been transmitted obscurely, because the doctrines of the Kabbala known only, in those early ages, to the adept, and the initiation, later on, of neophytes, was only yielded after a series of severe and terrible ordeals, whilst the revelation of its mysteries to the uninitiated was punished by death.

The necessity of silence was, in fact, one of the principal tenets of the Kabbala, and is represented in the figure of Adda-Nari,* by the position of the fingers of the hand holding the flowering branch of abundance; the thumb and the two first fingers, which in Chiromancy represent *will*,

An Arabic hand showing how all our fates are ruled by the zodiac.

Two alchemists ponder the mysteries of the astronomical spheres.

power, and *fatality*, are held open; whilst the third and fourth fingers, representing light and science, are closed. This was meant to indicate to the good—the initiated—that they would have, when united, strength and will to direct Fate; but that they must keep hidden from the wicked and ignorant both light and science. We must, however, in justice to the ancient Kabbalists, suggest that their inculcation of silence probably arose, not so much from a desire of domination, but rather from the fact that, feeling themselves superior in knowledge, they thought they were obeying a divine law in refusing to the wicked those lights which, when possessed by them, led, as perhaps they had sometimes found, to error. We, seeing things in the purer and clearer light of Christianity, give, or try to give, equal knowledge to all, without submitting the ignorant to the ordeal of initiation to prove their worthiness as recipients; but, after all, it amounts to much the same thing—give to all men truth and light in abundance, but all will not profit by it; we see this every day in our college system: the lesson is the same for all, but it is only the few who profit by it; and although we Christians appear to be obeying a divine law in opening the way of light and life—the life of knowledge to all, as God makes His sun to shine on good and bad equally, still we can, in some sort, understand the feeling of the ancient Magi, whose motto was: 'Know, Dare, Will, but keep Silence.'

* Adda-Nari, Nature—that is, the deity known under the name of Isis by the Egyptians.

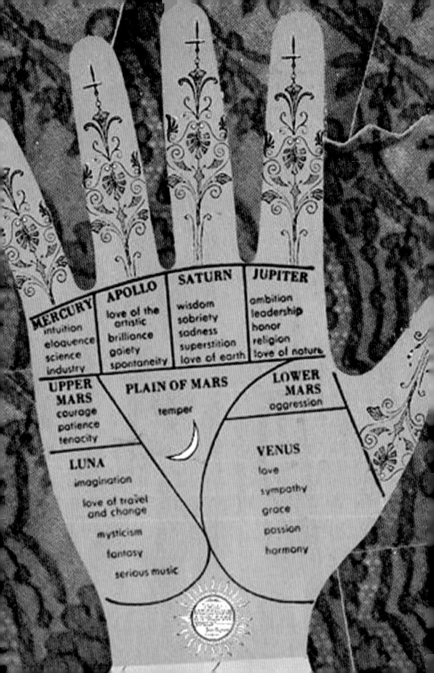

MERCURY
intuition
eloquence
science
industry

APOLLO
love of the
artistic
brilliance
gaiety
spontaneity

SATURN
wisdom
sobriety
sadness
superstition
love of earth

JUPITER
ambition
leadership
honor
religion
love of nature

UPPER MARS
courage
patience
tenacity

PLAIN OF MARS
temper

LOWER MARS
aggression

LUNA
imagination
love of travel
and change
mysticism
fantasy
serious music

VENUS
love
sympathy
grace
passion
harmony

Chapter II

The Mounts.

THE Kabbalists believed, as we have said, that each person was, throughout his existence, under the influence of the astral fluid of that planet which was in the ascendant at the moment of his birth, and that the life also received secondary influences from the other planets which were in conjunction with the planet dominant at that time. In their theory, Venus was supposed to be the most favourable planet; it is she who presides over the creation. Jupiter was also a happy planet, and its conjunction with Venus was favourable to the mortal born under the double influence. The junction of the Moon with Venus gives to those born under the double influence (especially if the Moon is the dominant planet) a melancholy, romantic temperament, physical beauty, and devotion of character. The junction of Mercury with Venus gives eloquence, gaiety, and tenderness. The union of Mars with Venus gives ardour, sensuality, and (when Mars is dominant) jealousy. The junction of the Sun with

The distribution of the mounts – how this compares with the topography of one's own palm speaks volumes.

Venus gives brightness, beauty, grace, and tenderness. Women born under this union charm without effort—they are beautiful, natural, and loving. So great is the favourable influence of Venus, that even that of the planet Saturn (supposed, when dominant, to have a fatal influence over a life) is mitigated by a junction with Venus at the time of birth.

Jupiter also, being a favourable planet, modifies the baleful influence of Saturn, which is the planet which represents Fatality, as that of Jupiter does Power.

We will not, however, enter into the various modifications resulting from all the different conjunctions, since to do so would form a little treatise of itself. It must, however, be borne in mind that each planet was supposed to bring its own influence and special qualities, and that the degrees of this admixture of qualities were (according to the Kabbalists) governed by the different degrees of ascendancy of each planet at the time of birth. The signs of these influences were supposed to be given in the hand and on the fingers, but more especially in the palm of the hand, where each line and mark was supposed to be the result of the passage of the several astral fluids emanating from the planet dominant, and those planets in conjunction with it, at the time of birth.

Having now landed ourselves (and, we trust, our readers with us) on the plain ground of Palmistry, we will proceed to describe that ancient belief in all its ramifications. With its aid the believers in it asserted the casting of the nativity to be needless, as, by simply examining a hand, they could, from the lines and marks upon it, at once indicate what planets had

*With Earth at the centre, this armillary sphere – or 'shadow clock'
– represents a fascinating sixteenth-century model of the universe.*

been in conjunction at the time of birth, and would, therefore, according to their theories, dominate the whole existence.

We do not pretend to any absolute belief in this science, as we do in that of graphology, on which we have written at some length,* but, having taken up the study from mere curiosity, we found it interesting, and, thinking it might be equally so to many others, we have epitomized the results of several years' study of the subject in these pages, which will, we trust, interest many readers.

In the plate belonging to this chapter (see opposite) we give a hand on which are marked the three principal lines of the palm, which are to be found, in a smaller or larger degree, in every hand, but which we have found vary, as regards their relative positions, in almost every hand, and we have (through the complaisance of friends) been allowed to examine some hundreds of palms since we first turned our attention to Palmistry. Of these three lines we shall now give some account. The first and largest, that which encircles the thumb, is called the Line of Life; by the length and evenness, or the reverse, of this line, the ancients held that the length of life was indicated, and also the illnesses and accidents by which that life was menaced in running its course. We shall enter more fully upon these marks further on; at present we merely wish to explain the plate belonging to this chapter. The line immediately above the Line of Life, and crossing the palm of the hand, is the Line of Head; by it we are to judge of the intellectual force of the owner of the hand. Above it is the Line of the Heart; from this we judge of the strength or the reverse of affection and tenderness in the nature.

* 'Indications of Character in Handwriting,' by R. Baughan.

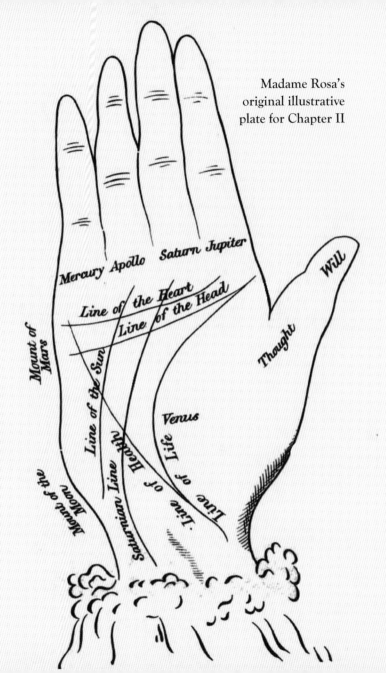

Madame Rosa's
original illustrative
plate for Chapter II

At the base of each finger there is a mount, more or less developed, on every hand. Now each of these mounts the ancients supposed to correspond with one of the planets from which it was believed to have more or less influence, according to its development, and the signs or marks to be found upon it.

It will be seen also, from the plate on page 23, that the ancients gave to each finger the name of one of the planets, thus:

The **first finger** represented Jupiter, the mount at its base being called the Mount of Jupiter.

The **second**, Saturn, the mount at its root being the Mount of Saturn.

The **third**, Apollo, the mount below being the Mount of Apollo.

The **fourth**, Mercury, the mount at its base being called the Mount of Mercury.

The **thumb** was sacred to Venus, and the root of the thumb was called the Mount of Venus.

It will also be seen that the planet Mars (although no finger is dedicated to it) is twice represented in the hand, along the side of the palm, by the Mount of Mars, and in the palm, between the Line of Life and the Line of the Head, which is called the Plain of Mars.

The Moon is only represented by the Mount of the Moon, at the lower part of the palm, on the opposite side of the hand to the thumb.

When these mounts are well in their places, and clearly, but not too strongly defined, they give the qualities of the planet

A page from Antropologium de hominis dignitate, *published by German philosopher Magnus Hundt in 1501.*

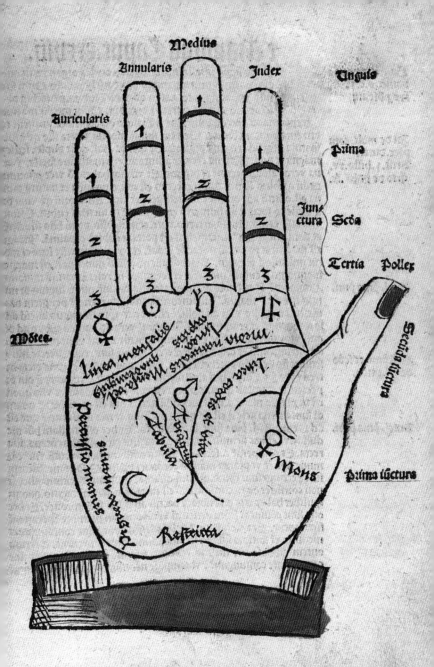

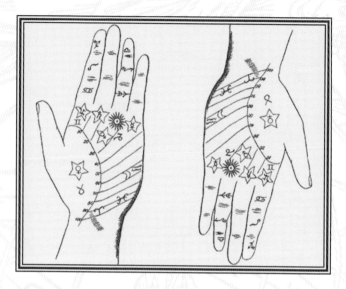

*'Chiromancy is nearly as ancient as astrology, with which it is indissolubly connected':
a diagram from inside Mme Rosa's study,* The Influence of the Stars, *1904.*

they represent; but when any mount is not well marked, or even, as frequently happens, is quite deficient, there is, according to the Chiromancists, a want of the qualities shown to exist where the mount is clearly defined. If the mounts are not only ill-defined, but represented by a cavity, that cavity would indicate the existence of qualities which are the reverse of those indicated by the mount; whereas an exceeding development would denote an excess of the qualities given by the mount.

Thus the Mount of Jupiter, which is immediately under the index, is supposed, when fairly developed, to indicate noble ambition, love of nature, kindliness, generosity, religion, and happy marriage. When in excess—that is, when the mount is so large as to invade that next it, the Mount of Saturn—it indicates superstition, exaggerated pride, and domineering self-assertion. The total absence of this mount (which is sometimes, but rarely, seen) indicates coldness, selfishness, irreligion, and that want of dignity which is produced by the utter absence of self-respect.

The Mount of Saturn is found immediately beneath the second finger, which the ancients assigned to Saturn, the planet of Fatality. Saturn was supposed to give extreme misfortune, or extreme good fortune, according to the development of the mount and the signs and lines to be seen upon it, and the course of the Saturnian Line, or Line of Fate (of which we shall speak further on), in the palm of the hand.

Saturn was supposed to give, when well developed, prudence, wisdom, and, to a certain extent, success; when in excess it gives sadness, taciturnity, asceticism, dread of the after life, and yet sometimes a predisposition to suicide. The total absence of the mount indicates an insignificant existence.

The Mount of Apollo is placed at the root of the third finger, which was sacred to Apollo, or the sun; when this mount is well developed it indicates love of art and literature, which shows itself (according to temperament) in poetry, painting, sculpture, or music; it gives also religion of the aesthetic tolerant sort, grace, riches, and celebrity; in excess it gives love of show, frivolity, and vaingloriousness. The total absence of the mount means a thoroughly material existence; absence of all taste for art—a life without colour, a day without sunlight!

The Mount of Mercury is found at the base of the fourth finger, and, when well-defined, indicates intelligence, success in science, and even in occult studies; the love of work,

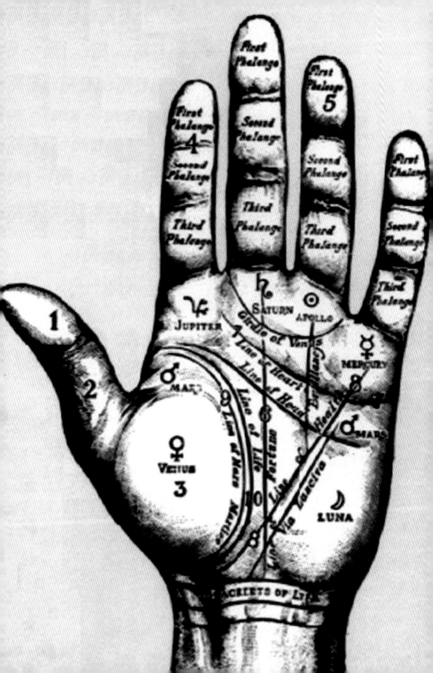

activity both of mind and body, and eloquence; in excess it gives impudence, theft, and falsehood; the absence of the mount indicates no aptitude for science, no intellectuality, a negative existence. Of course, if the Mount of Apollo is well-defined, the last quality would be over-ridden by the success which the Mount of Apollo indicates.

The Mount of Mars is at the side of the hand, opposite the thumb, just below the Mount of Mercury, and when well-developed, indicates courage, ardour and resolution; in excess it gives cruelty, anger, revenge and tyranny; the absence of the mount gives cowardice and want of self-command.

The Mount of the Moon is found immediately below that of Mars, and when well developed, gives imagination of the dreamy sentimental order, gentle melancholy, and love of solitude; in excess, it gives morbid melancholy, caprice, fantastic imagination; the absence of the mount indicates want of poetry in the nature, positivism.

The Mount of Venus, which is formed by the root of the thumb, indicates when fairly developed, love of the beautiful, melody in music, the desire of pleasing, and sensuous tenderness; in excess, it gives love of material pleasures, coquetry, inconstancy and (when other signs, afterwards to be explained, are also seen in the hand) extreme sensuality.

This map of the hand appeared in an advert for Sunlight Soap in 1892.

Chapter III.

The Line of Life.

OUR last chapter contained a sketch of a hand (see page 23), on which not only were traced the three primary lines of the palm; that is, the lines which are found, more or less marked, in every hand, even in that of a newly-born infant; but also the Saturnian Line; the Line of the Sun, and the Line of Health, which are not always found on every hand. We will now give an ampler description of each of these lines:

We will begin with the Line of Life, which the ancients divided into ten compartments (see large plate on page 33), each representing ten years, and thus they were enabled, they thought, to prognosticate at what epoch in a life the illnesses or dangers, indicated by the form or colour of the line, would be likely to occur. It will be noticed that the ancients made the life take its course up to ten years of age, from Jupiter (Divinity) to Apollo (Light), and that they made the space occupied by the first ten years larger than those

A dream-like sketch by Parisian artist
Eugene Lacoste (1818-1908).

representing the succeeding decades in the life. The spaces from ten to sixty years are of equal size, but, as the vital force then retrogrades, the ancients supposed the fluid to be less plentiful, and, when the life reaches eighty years, it will be seen that, acting on the same reasoning, they made the spaces still more compressed.

When the Line of Life is long, well-formed, slightly coloured, and goes all round the thumb, it indicates a long life and free from serious illness; but when the line is wide and pale in colour, it indicates bad health; when it is short, it means early death.

If the Line of Life is broken on one hand, but is marked in a continuous line on the other, these signs indicate an illness of a very serious nature; but if the broken line should appear in *both* hands, it means death at the epoch corresponding with the place on the line where the break occurs. When the Line of Life is not clearly defined, but is formed by a sort of chain of small lines, it indicates continuous small illnesses.

When the Line of Life, instead of starting from the side of the hand, takes its rise in the Mount of Jupiter, which is sometimes, but rarely, the case, it is supposed to indicate a life of successful ambition, honours and celebrity—qualities given by the influence of Jupiter.

If the Line of Life joins the Line of the Heart, or the Line of the Head, it indicates grave misfortune or violent death, by which the ancients probably meant to infer that when either the heart or the head is dominated by merely vital instincts, the life is menaced by misfortune; but, when the Line of Life is very far from the Line of Head, it indicates a life that accomplishes its course without much intelligence;

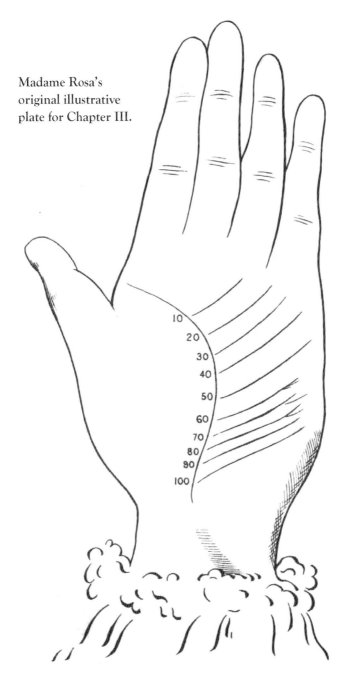

Madame Rosa's original illustrative plate for Chapter III.

10
20
30
40
50
60
70
80
90
100

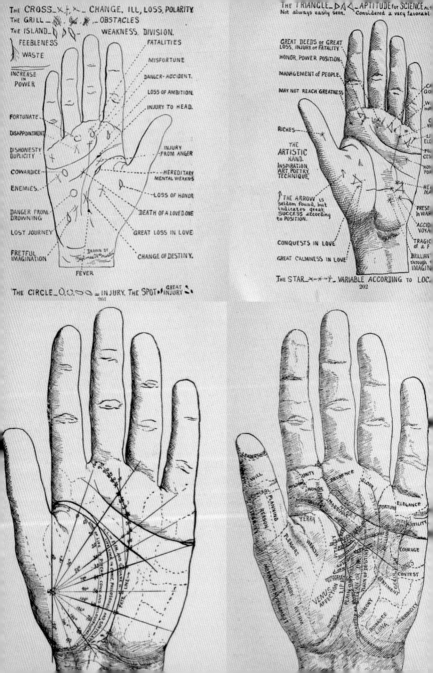

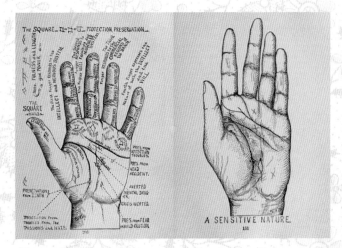

Left and above: *Various attempts by thinkers, philosophers and artists throughout the ages to map the mysteries of the palm.*

so also, if the Line of Life is very far from the Line of Heart, it indicates a life without love.

When the Line of Life is bi-forked at its termination, near the wrist, it means a total change in the way of life towards its close, and, should one of the branches tend towards the Mount of the Moon, it indicates madness towards the end of existence. A double Line of Life is sometimes, but rarely, seen; this indicates excess of health and long life.

When the Line of Life throws branches upwards towards the Plain of Mars, it was supposed to mean that, after long struggles, riches and honours would be acquired in old age.

THE WONDERS
IN WHICH HE IS TOLD THAT HE WILL MARRY A BLON

Chapter IV.

The Line of Heart and Line of Head.

THE Line of Heart is placed immediately beneath the mounts at the root of each finger. This line, when clear, straight, and well-coloured, rising in the Mount of Jupiter and extending to the outer edge of the hand, signifies that its possessor has a good heart capable of strong affection. If, instead of commencing on the Mount of Jupiter, it does not take its rise till the Mount of Saturn, then the love will, in that nature, be rather of a sensual character. We have sometimes seen the Line of Heart stretch across the whole of the hand; such a line announces a too great amount of tenderness—a passionate and blind devotion in affection.

When the Line of Heart is broken in several places, it means inconstancy, both in love and friendship. Should the breaks be seen immediately beneath the Mount of Saturn,

'The Wonders of Palmistry,' a pen-and-ink
drawing by Charles Dana Gibson, 1897.

STRY.

HIM, BUT HE WILL HAVE TO SPEAK QUICK.

it indicates a tragic end to the love; if beneath the Mount of Apollo, by pride; but if between the Mounts of Saturn and Apollo, the heart-break will be occasioned by folly; if between the Mounts of Apollo and Mercury, by cupidity—the desire to make a better marriage in a worldly point of view; if the break occurs immediately beneath the Mount of Mercury, the evil issue of the love will be from caprice.

When the Line of the Heart appears in the form of the links of a chain instead of in one clear line, it indicates inconstancy and indecision—a tendency towards a series of *amourettes* rather than to a high and serious affection.

The Line of Heart of a deep-red colour indicates a power of love ardent even to violence; but when, on the contrary, the Line of Heart is pale and wide, it is an indication of coldness of temperament.

When, at its starting-point, the Line of Heart is seen to turn round the base of the Mount of Jupiter somewhat in the form of a circle, it is what the ancient Chiromancists called 'Solomon's Ring,' and indicates an aptitude for the occult sciences. If the Line of Heart joins the Line of Life between the thumb and forefinger, it is a sign (if the mark is in *both* hands) of a violent death; if only in one, of a serious, but not fatal, illness connected with the heart.

If the Line of Heart droops towards the Line of Head and touches it, it is a sign of coldness and calculation in the affections; the instincts of the heart are dominated by worldly considerations.

If the Line of Heart is intersected by other lines, it is

The delicate palm of Napoleon's wayward wife, Joséphine de Beauharnais, as captured by cartomancer Le Normand in 1827.

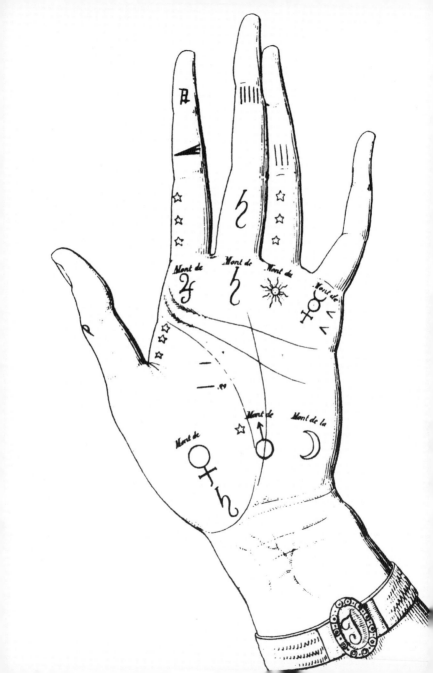

supposed to indicate as many troubles in the affections as there are crossings to be discerned. *Red* punctures on the Line of Heart mean as many wounds as there are punctures;* but *white* spots on the line indicate as many conquests in love as there are white spots on the line.

If, on starting, the Line of the Heart is bi-forked, and one branch of the fork rises towards the Mount of Jupiter, it indicates great happiness of a glorious nature; but if the other branch stops between the finger of Jupiter and that of Saturn, it is merely negative happiness—a life passed without great misfortunes. When a hand (but this is rare) is entirely without the Line of Heart, it would indicate an iron will, wickedness, and cruelty.

The Line of the Head rises between the Line of Life and the Mount of Jupiter, and when it is long and clear it denotes a sound judgment and masterly intellect; but it must not extend straight across the hand, as that signifies a disposition to avarice, or at any rate to extreme economy, because unless corrected by a rich Line of Heart, it would indicate an excess of calculation in the character.

If the Line of Head is long, but droops towards the Mount of the Moon, it signifies ideality in excess. Life and its numerous duties and cares will be considered from an artistic and unreal point of view, for the Mount of the Moon, it will be remembered, represents imagination in excess, romanticism, and superstition; and if the Line of the Head droops very low to the Mount of the Moon, it indicates more than superstition—it is then mysticism.

If, instead of drooping towards the Mount of the Moon, the Line of Head rises towards the mounts at its close, the intellect will partake of the qualities of that mount towards which it rises: thus, if it rises beneath the Mount of Mercury, the intellect will be employed successfully in commerce; if towards Apollo, in art and literature.

The Line of the Head pale-coloured and wide indicates a want of intelligence; so also does a very short line, only extending half-way across the hand. This we have often seen in persons of medium intellect.

The Line of the Head broken in two immediately under the Mount of Saturn means, where the sign is on both hands, death on the scaffold, or at least a fatal wound on the head. When this sign appears in only one hand (no matter which), it indicates a probability of madness from an unfortunate passion.

If the Line of the Head is long, thin, and not deeply marked, it shows infidelity and treachery. If, towards its close, it mounts suddenly to the Line of the Heart, it signifies early death.

When the Line of the Head is not joined to the Line of Life at its starting-point, it indicates jealousy and untruth. If large, round, red spots are seen on the Line of Head, they indicate so many wounds on the head; whilst white spots on the Line of the Head indicate as many successes in literature as there are spots to be seen.

* If the puncture is beneath the finger of Saturn, the evil will come from a practical person; if under Apollo, from an artist; if under Mercury, from a lawyer or doctor.

MAGIE CELES
SUCCÈS
GLOIRE
5
TRIOMPHE RENOMMÉE
CHANGEMENT
DÉPLACEMENT
4
ÉCONOMIE
INTÉRIEURE
6
TRAVAIL, BONNE CONDUITE
VI
IV
INDUSTRIE
3
AFFAIRES
ACCORD
SYMPATHIE
7
BONNE UNION DES CŒURS
SCIENCE
CHIROMANCIE ASTROLOGIQUE & PHYSIOLOGIQUE.
MAIN DE GÉNIE
VII
JEU NOUVEAU DE BONNE AVENTURE
par les Mains
TRAHISON
III
II
8
JUSTICE
DOMINATION
AUTORITÉ
DU POUVOIR
9
LOI
I
V
POSITION
RICHESSE
12
BIEN-ÊTRE
FATALITÉ
de la chance
DOMINATION
ou du hasard
10
FORCE MAJEURE
SAGESSE
de Parents
ou de gens
DIRECTION
de Vieillards
d'expérience
11

Chapter V

The Saturnian Line.

THE Saturnian Line, or Line of Fate, overrides the Mount of Saturn, and generally penetrates to the root of the second finger. This line has, in different hands, a different point of departure. Sometimes it rises in the Line of Life, in which case its indications participate in those of the Line of Life in the same hand; sometimes it takes its rise in the Plain of Mars, in which case it announces a troubled life, and still more so when it penetrates beyond the root of the finger of Saturn, and reaches the first joint. When it starts from the Mount of the Moon it signifies happiness, which is the result of a strong affection; if, however, the Saturnian Line, rising in the Mount of the Moon, stops short at the Line of the Heart, it is happiness crushed by an unfortunate attachment or physical disease of the heart. When the Saturnian Line starts from the wrist, exactly below the finger of Saturn, and goes in a direct line to it, cutting through the mount,

Back in the late nineteenth century, A. de Para d'Hermès devised this divinatory palm-reading game.

but stopping at the root of the finger, it is a sign of a life of extreme happiness. If the Saturnian Line stops short at the Line of Head, it is misfortune in affairs through a false calculation; or, taken in conjunction with a troubled Line of Life, it would mean a physical brain affection.

If the Saturnian Line is straight and well-coloured at its termination—that is, as it nears the finger of Saturn—it indicates happiness and riches in old age, however troubled the life may have been before.

This 1620 diagram – taken from Robert Fludd's controversial Utriusque Cosmi *– shows long-forgotten names for each of our fingers.*

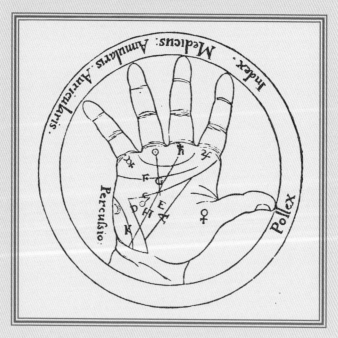

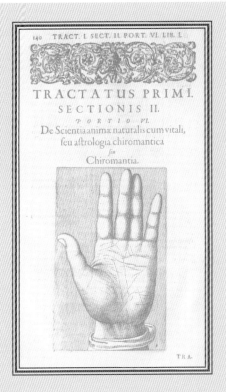

Stranger than fiction: an intriguing page from inside Fludd's Utriusque Cosmi.

If the Saturnian Line is broken and irregular, it means trouble and worry in life; and according to whether these breaks occur on the Line of Head or on the Line of Heart, so will the troubles be of the head or heart—troubles arising from affairs or the affections. If the Line of Life is irregular, denoting uncertain health, these troubles may be physical evils to the heart or head.

The Saturnian Line does not always go direct to the finger of Saturn; it is often seen mounting to the finger of Mercury, when it indicates success in commerce, science, or oratory. If its course goes towards Jupiter, it signifies happiness obtained through satisfied pride and ambition; if to Apollo, success in art, celebrity, and riches.

If the Saturnian Line is twisted in a sort of spiral at the starting-point, but yet the upper part of it goes in a clear, direct line to the Mount of Saturn, and cuts through it to the root of the finger without penetrating beyond, it indicates

The ancient arts of divination – whether by playing cards, the zodiac or the palm – are more closely related than one would imagine, as illustrated by this chart.

At the heart of the Golden Wheel of fortune lies the palm.

a troubled and anxious youth followed by riches and good fortune in middle age. If the twisted line continues, and crosses the Line of the Head and the Line of Heart, the troubles will continue until old age, and the good fortune be only quite at the close of life.

If the Mount of Saturn is much wrinkled, and the Saturnian Line cuts through it, and is of a deep-red colour, and mounts as high as the third joint of the finger of Saturn, it indicates a violent and disgraceful end—death on the gallows.

There are some hands in which the Saturnian Line is very faintly indicated, and when this is the case it signifies an uneventful, insignificant existence. The Esquimaux, for example, who live in a wretched climate, and have hard, unlovely lives, have absolutely, some of them, *no* Saturnian Line in their hands; and M. Serres, a famous French anthropologist, asserts that this line (which he calls the Caucasian Line) is only to be found in the hands of the white races; whilst M. Desbarolles, another French writer on this subject, goes farther, and affirms that, among persons condemned to a dry, unintellectual, vegetative life, even among the white races, the Saturnian Line is often found entirely wanting.

The Saturnian Line is one of great importance according to Chiromancists, for it corrects and modifies the significations both of the lines and of the mounts. A double Saturnian Line, which is sometimes, but very rarely, seen, indicates great moral corruption and physical infirmities, brought about by the abuse of material pleasures.

Lines of the closed hand, as depicted in L'Art de Chyromance Lyons *by Andre Corvo, circa 1545.*

Signs of the Zodiac in the Hand

Chapter VI.

The Line of the Sun and Line of Health.

THE Line of the Sun takes its rise either in the Line of Life or from the Mount of the Moon, and, ascending, it traces a furrow in the Mount of Apollo, but stops at the root of the finger; it signifies, when straight and well defined, and taking the course we have described, celebrity in literature or art, whether in poetry, painting, sculpture, or music. Those having the Line of Sun thus traced, even who are not artists by profession, and whom destiny has placed in quite inartistic careers, will always have artistic tastes, eye for colour, ear for music, or a perception of beauty in form or in language.

If the Line of the Sun subdivides, in traversing the Mount of Apollo, into several lines, it indicates a tendency to cultivate several branches of art, which prevents the success which generally crowns excess of artistic feeling when

'Signs of the Zodiac on the Hand,'
painted by Nadia Turner.

A medieval manuscript telling of the curious sciences of astrology and divination, 1717.

confined in its expression to one especial art; it also indicates too great a struggle after effect in art; it is more significative of the dilettante, or patron of art generally, than the artist *pur et simple*. When the Line of the Sun, in its upward course, is barred by several transverse lines, there are obstacles in the career of art; but if the line continues, and marks a single deep furrow in the mount till it reaches the root of the finger, these obstacles will, in the end, be conquered, and success, riches, honours, and celebrity will be attained.

An illustrative plate from Edward Heron-Allen's Manual of Cheirosophy, 1885.

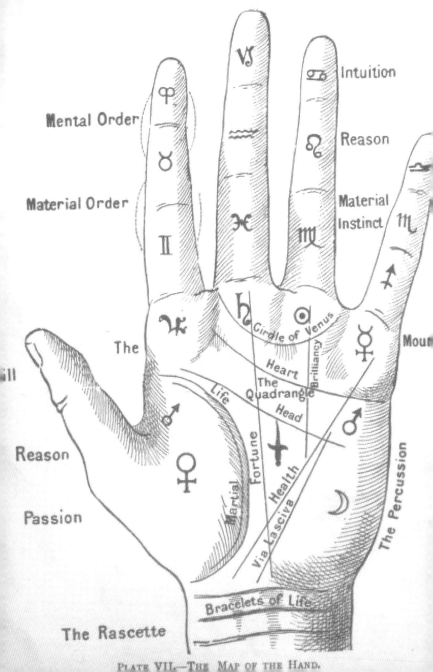

PLATE VII.—THE MAP OF THE HAND.

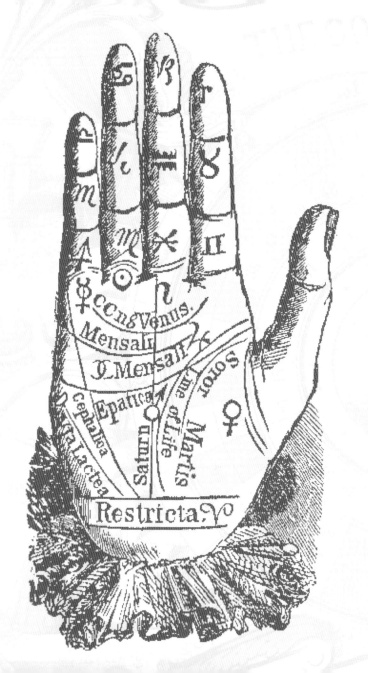

The Line of Health (which we are about to describe) and the Line of the Sun, do not appear in every hand, and the Saturnian Line, though very important, as we have explained, because it modifies the effects of both lines and mounts, is sometimes only faintly discernible.

The Line of Health, or, as it is sometimes called, the Line of the Liver, takes its rise at the wrist, near the Line of Life, and mounts in the direction of the Mount of Mercury. If it is well coloured and the line is not broken, it denotes good health, great power of memory, and success in business pursuits; if the line becomes broken, or is forked at its close, before it reaches the mount, it indicates severe illness in old age. If the line is unequally coloured, and gets redder as it crosses the Line of Head, it indicates a predisposition to apoplexy; if it stops suddenly on the Line of the Heart, a serious physical heart affection.

The Line of Health is sometimes, but rarely, accompanied by another line called by Chiromancists the Milky Way; when this line commences side by side with the Line of Health, and mounts with it, in an unbroken line, towards the finger of Mercury, it signifies a long life of uninterrupted happiness. This line, which is sometimes called the Via lasciva, gives ardour in love, because a superabundance of health gives force to passion.

An illustration from inside The Witches' Dream Book and Fortune Teller, *1885.*

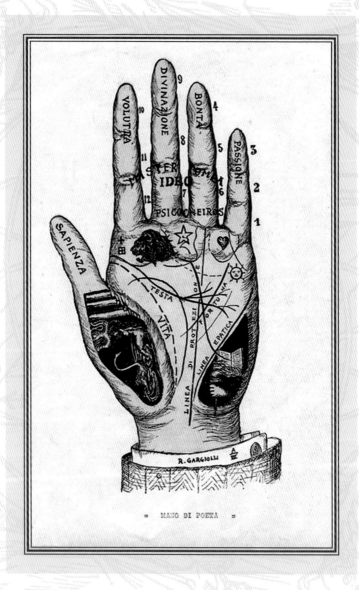

= MANO DI POETA =

Chapter VII.

Concerning the Ring of Venus, and the Lines to be Found on the Wrist, and the Letter M. to be Seen in Most Hands.

THE Ring of Venus seems to enclose, as in an island, the Mounts of Saturn and Apollo; this line is not seen in many hands, and, when fully developed, signifies unbridled passion and debauchery of all kinds when, in conjunction with it, the Mount of Venus is strongly developed and marked with crossway lines. If, with the signs mentioned above, the Ring of Venus is strongly marked, yet *broken* at its centre in *both* hands, it is a sign of eccentric and depraved passion; still, there are always modifications of these bad signs, and a very good Line

This richly detailed hand by R. Gargiolli shows us the temperament 'di poeta' (of the poet).

of Head would, by bringing reason to bear upon passion, considerably mitigate the evil indications of the broken ring.

Sometimes the Ring of Venus will be seen to ascend and lose itself on the Mount of Mercury, leaving one end of the semicircle open, in which case science and industry mitigate, in some sort, the terribly strong instincts of voluptuousness indicated by this mark ; but if, on contrary, the semi-circle, after extending itself to the Mount of Mercury, closes itself at the root of the finger, such a mark in the hand would indicate a terrible and absorbing power of passion, which would not hesitate at any means to secure its end. A line traced on the wrist is a sign of long life, above all if there are three of these lines, as is sometimes seen, a triple bracelet. These lines indicate, in Chiromancy, thirty years of life each, and the three lines form what is called the magic bracelet, indicating long life, health, and riches. If these lines are formed irregularly, like the links of a chain, and more especially if the first one—that next the hand—is so formed, it indicates a long life of labour, but acquiring ease and competency at its close. If a cross appears in the centre of the wrist, it indicates a rich heritage at the close of life. When lines start upwards from the bracelet, and ascend towards the Mount of the Moon, they denote as many voyages by water as there are lines. If a line starts from the wrist, and, after traversing the Plain of Mars, goes to the Mount of Apollo, such a line presages riches and honours coming from royalty.

A line starting from the wrist, and going direct to the Mount of Saturn, announces long travels by land.

A glimpse into Les mystères de la main, *written by Adolphe Desbarrolles in 1860.*

traverser horizontalement la main et entourer complé-
tement le mont de Mercure.

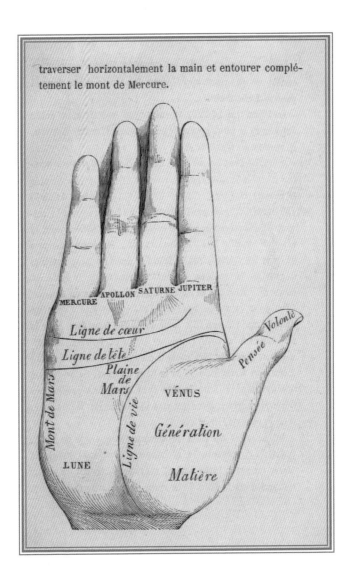

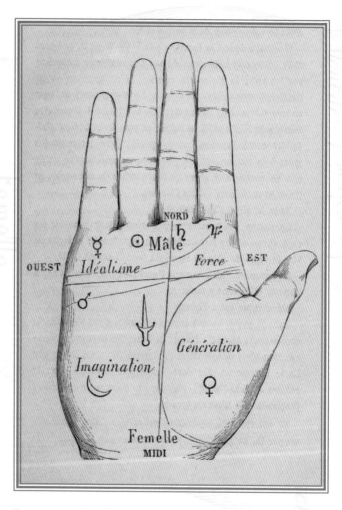

Encompassing male and female, east and west, this palm from
Les mystères de la main *shows a delicate balance of opposites.*

The letter M, formed more or less regularly in every hand by the Line of Life, the Line of Head, and the Line of Heart, represents the three worlds: the material, the natural, and the divine.

The first, the Line of Life, surrounds Love and Generation, as represented by the thumb, which is, as we have seen, sacred to Venus—the material world, or world of sense—but the Mount of Venus may either degenerate love to vice, or perfectionate it to tenderness. With high instincts the Mount of Venus is a good quality, for, *without it*, all the other passions are hard and selfish.

The second line—the Line of the Head—stretches across the natural world; it traverses the Plain and the Mount of Mars, which represent the struggle of Love and Reason in existence—the natural world, life as it presents itself to most persons. There is in the hand the Plain of Mars and the Mount of Mars; both mean a struggle; the mount is the struggle of resistance; the Plain of Mars is the struggle of aggression.

The third line, that of the heart, encloses the divine world, for it surrounds the mounts which represent Religion, Jupiter; Fate, Saturn; Art, Apollo or the Sun; Science, Mercury; all of which were supposed by the ancients to be especially influenced by the astral light, or fluid, emanating from the planets.

According to the proportions—the relative proportions—which these three lines bear to one another, so the life was supposed to be influenced by the three different worlds represented. Thus we have a hand in which material (sensual) pleasure dominates; the line of the material world enclosing a space greatly superior to that of the two others. We think

it needless to give further examples of these differences, for, after all, this matter is but a *résumé* of what has been said before about the power of correction which one line has over the other. Given a wide range to sensual pleasure in the hand, but a good and extensive Line of the Head, the former will be corrected by it, as reason dominates passion; or given the strong powers of sensuality, with a wide range to the divine world by the space occupied between the Line of Heart and the mounts, and again, religion, love of art and science, will correct and keep under extreme sensuality. In judging of the hand, each line must be considered with reference to the others, and the hand must be considered in all its bearings, before an opinion on the tendencies it indicates can be arrived at with any degree of correctness.

Isis – as depicted in Les mystères de la main. *The lingam emblazoned on her forehead is a powerful symbol of creative energy.*

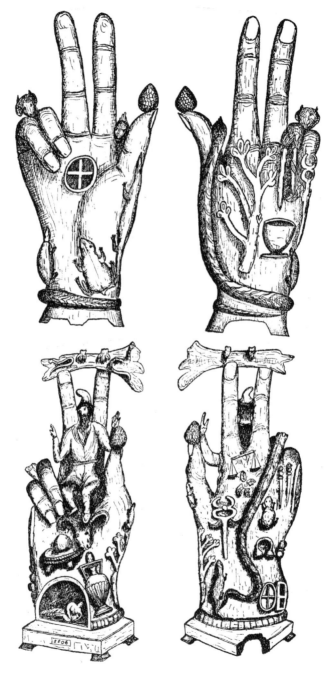

Chapter VIII.

Of Signs On The Hand.

WE have now spoken of all the lines of the palm, *viz.*: the Line of Life; the Line of the Head; the Line of the Heart; the Line of Fate, or Saturnian Line; the Line of the Sun, or, as it is sometimes called, the Line of Art; the Line of Health, and of its sister line, the Milky Way. We have also described all the mounts, and the qualities inspired by the astral influences indicated by the greater or lesser development of these mounts; but there are other signs on the hand which were supposed to modify the qualities of the several mounts, or exaggerate them into vices, and it is of these signs we will, in this chapter, treat.

A star (fig. 1 on page 67) indicates something beyond our own power of action—a fatality for good or evil over which we have, personally, no power. A star on the Mount of Jupiter indicates honours, great and unexpected glory, for Jupiter is always a favourable planet.

The significance of these statuettes – shown in F.T. Elworthy's 1900 tome, Horns of Honour – is still a mystery, but there's no doubt they were used to magical ends . . .

A star on the Mount of Saturn means assassination or death on the scaffold.

A star on the Mount of Apollo indicates fatal riches—fortune which brings with it unhappiness.

A star on the Mount of Mercury indicates dishonour—a proneness to theft.

A star on the Mount of the Moon means danger of drowning; the Moon has power over the sea.

A star on Venus means unhappiness caused by love.

A square (fig. 2, opposite) announces power and energy of the mount on which it is found, except upon Venus, when it infers imprisonment.

A circle (fig. 3, opposite) on any of the mounts, but above all on the Mount of Apollo, signifies success in the qualities given by the mount on which it appears; but a circle on the lines of the hand has always a bad signification. A circle on the Line of Life means loss of one eye, and two circles would indicate total blindness.

An island (fig. 4, opposite), is again always a bad sign: on the Line of Heart it signifies adultery; on the Line of Life, mystery or dishonourable birth; on the Line of Head, ruin arising from fraudulent speculations; on the Line of Health, disorders of the liver and the digestion; on the Saturnian Line, an island indicates happiness from an adulterous liaison; but if the island is broken in shape, it indicates poignant grief arising from an illicit affection.

The lines which are found going lengthways round the side of the hand between the Line of Heart and the root of the finger of Mercury, denote the number of marriages a person will form in life, or the number of serious attachments; and

Madame Rosa's original
illustrative plate for Chapter VIII.

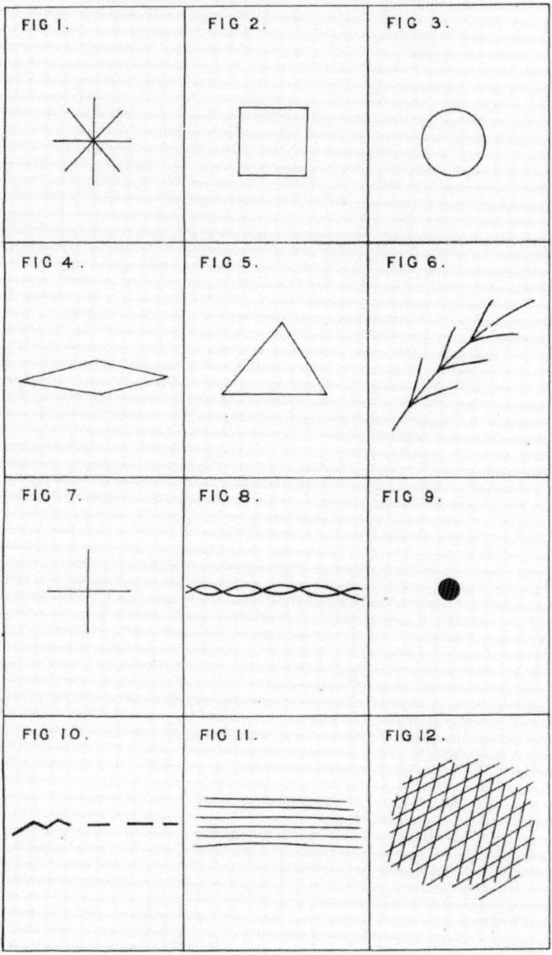

FIG 1.	FIG 2.	FIG 3.
FIG 4.	FIG 5.	FIG 6.
FIG 7.	FIG 8.	FIG 9.
FIG 10.	FIG 11.	FIG 12.

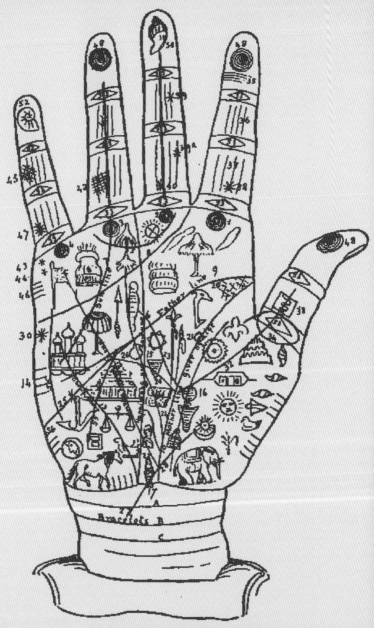

PLATE I.—THE REFERENCE HAND.

if these marks take the form of islands, the marriages will be with cousins or very near relatives.

A triangle (fig. 5, page 67), announces aptitudes, and has always a favourable signification; on the Mount of Jupiter it signifies diplomatic distinction; on Saturn, a man given to the study of mystic science, and distinguished in his acquirements of it; on the Mount of Apollo, it indicates success in art or literature; on Mars, military glory; on the Mount of the Moon, mysticism; on the Mount of Venus, prudence in love; on Mercury, great aptitude and distinction in science, or in one of the learned professions.

A branch (fig. 6, page 67), on any of the mounts or lines, announces excess of the qualities indicated by the mount or line on which it appears; but it is generally seen on the lines: on the Line of Heart it means warmth of affection and excess of devotion, extreme unselfishness; on the Line of Head, great intelligence; on the Line of Life, or on the Line of Health—in either case, exuberance of health and long life; on the Saturnian Line, great happiness.

A cross (fig. 7, page 67) is generally an unfavourable sign; but on the Mount of Jupiter it means a love marriage, and consequently generally a happy marriage.

A cross in the centre of the hand, between the Line of Head and the Line of Heart, is superstition; or at any rate, even with a good Line of Head, it would indicate love of occult science and mysticism.

A cross on the Mount of Saturn is fatality, and announces the vehement influence of this melancholy planet.

An 1895 engraving with palpable
Eastern influence and Indian spice.

A cross on the Mount of Apollo indicates a serious check in the career of art.

A cross on the Mount of Mercury means perjury and deceit, and (like the star) a predisposition to theft.

A cross on the Plain of Mars indicates a combative nature.

A cross in the base of the triangle formed by the Plain of Mars and the Mounts of Venus and the Moon indicates an event of great importance, late in life, which will change the whole tenour of existence.

A cross on the Mount of the Moon indicates a man so untrue, that he will lie even to himself.

A cross on the Mount of Venus indicates a single but fatal attachment, unless, on the same hand, the cross is seen on the Mount of Jupiter, indicating a love marriage, when it only deepens the force of the happy omen.

Chains (fig. 8, page 67) always mean obstacles and worries which prevent the free action of the good effects of the lines on which they appear; they must not, however, be confused with islands, which have much the same form, but are much larger, and always appear singly. Chains are most generally seen on the Saturnian Line, when they mean pecuniary worries, more especially, unless they appear just as the line is crossing the Line of Heart, when they would indicate anxiety and sorrow through the affections.

A spot (fig. 9 page 67) is sometimes favourable and sometimes the reverse. Red spots on the Line of Heart mean physical ills of the heart. White spots mean as many love conquests as there are spots. On the Line of Head, if *red*, they mean physical accidents to the head; but if white, they indicate, if under the Mount of Mercury, scientific discoveries;

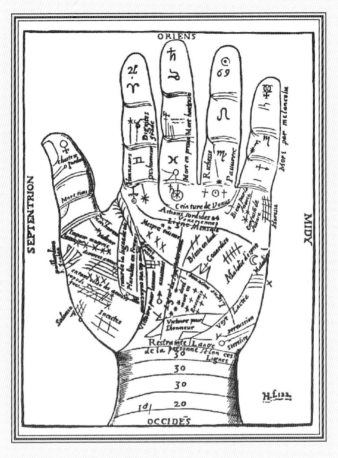

Mapping the future is an exact science in this uniquely detailed plate from Jean Belot's 1649 Oeuvres.

if under Apollo, success in literature; if under Saturn, success in pecuniary matters through intelligent speculation. Curved

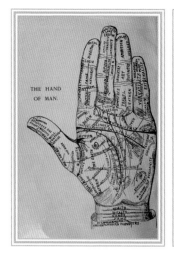

THE HAND
OF MAN.

YOUR FATE IS
IN YOUR HAND.

These illustrations from Louis Williams' Key to Palmistry, 1902, provide crucial clues in unlocking the secrets of one's fate.

and broken lines (see fig. 10, page 67) mean disasters wherever they are seen; on the Line of Head madness, more especially if the line droops towards the Mount of the Moon.

Hair-lines (fig. 11, page 67) show an excess of the quality of the line, but their very excess sometimes leads to failure. The people who have these lines on their hands frequently, in acts of kindness, overstep the mark. Talleyrand must have had such people in his mind when he said, '*Surtout point de zèle.*'

Cross-bars (fig. 12, page 67) are always obstacles, but on different parts of the hand they have different significations. On the mounts they give excess of the qualities. For instance, on the Mount of Jupiter, religion degenerates into superstition, and self-respect into dominating self-assertion and tyranny; on the Mount of Saturn the cross-bars give excess of misfortune; on the Mount of Apollo, folly, vanity, and error; on the Mount of Mercury, cunning, deceit, and theft; on the Mount of Mars, violent death; on the Mount of the Moon, inquietude, discontent, and morbid imagination, which always sees the sad side of everything.

Cross-bars on the Mount of Venus mean lasciviousness and obscenity, unless the Lines of Head and Heart are both good, and then the cross-bars on the Mount of Venus would merely indicate a very ardent and passionate interest in the opposite sex.

Lines going upwards from any line are good, and increase the good qualities of the line they accompany. A line going direct from the Mount of Venus to that of Mercury is the union of Mercury and Venus, and means love and fortune.

Although the science of Palmistry would seem to be confined to the study of the lines of the palm of the hand, as the shape and relative proportions of the fingers to the palm are supposed to modify the indications given by the lines and mounts, it may be as well to give a short account of their supplementary signs. When the fingers are shorter than the palm, and thick at their base, it indicates a sensuous nature; but this may, again, be modified by a good Line of Head, which would give the prudence which would hold in check the too great tendency to material pleasures.

Long, taper fingers show artistic feeling, romance, and a certain amount of idleness.

Short fingers, but with pointed tips, show love of detail. People with these hands seldom take a broad view of matters, but they have a strong feeling for beauty, and are generally lovers of art, if not artists themselves.

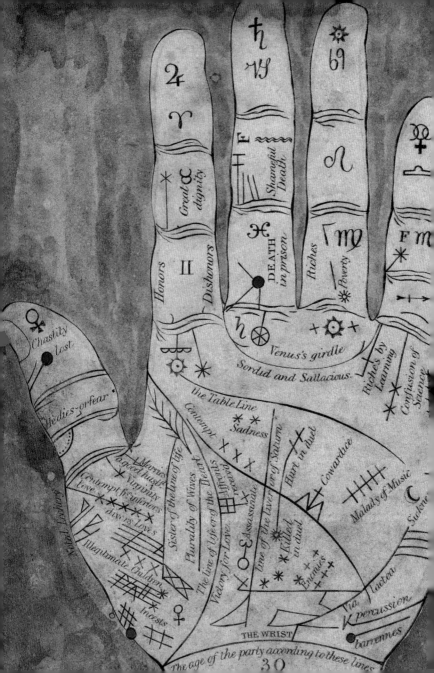

Chastity
lost

He dies or fear

♀ Chastity
lost

Honors

Ⅱ

Dishonors

Great ♎ dignity

♃
♈
✳

♄
♑

☉
♋

F
♒ Shameful Death

DEATH
in prison ♓

Riches ♍

Poverty

F M
♏

Riches by Learning

Confusion of Science

Venus's girdle

♄ ⊕ ✕ ☉ ✕

Sordid and Sallacious

the Table Line

Contempt

Sadness

Hurt in duel

Cowardice

Malady of Music

Suden

Marries
to good husb.
Virginity

Contempt of inferiors
Love Contempt of inferiors
divers Loves

No of Embarys

Illegitimate Children

Sister of the lines of life

Plurality of Wives

Victory for Love

The line of Liser of the Beaux

friends
received

Assassinate

Line of the Liser of Saturn

Killed
in duel

Enemies

Incests ♀

Via Lactea

Percussion

barrennes

THE WRIST

The age of the party according to these lines

30

Straight fingers, square at the tips, show reason, order, and calm, dispassionate, broad views on all subjects.

Fingers spatulated at their tips (that is, having the flesh growing round the nails, which in such hands are generally short and flat), show activity, ardour, movement.

Fingers large at the joints show a philosophical turn of mind.

If the first joint of the thumb is long, it announces a powerful will; if the second, great reasoning powers. Thus a long thumb always shows force of character; but a long thumb, in which the first joint is disproportionately long as regards the second, indicates a stubborn and senseless will, unchecked by reason—stupid obstinacy, in fact. A short thumb shows a weak, characterless person, unless a strong Line of Head corrects this want of force in the nature; then it might mean a highly intellectual person, but one who, from *insouciance* of character, was easily led. Many poets have short thumbs, but then, in conjunction with this sign of weakness, we invariably find with them a long Line of Head, drooping towards the Mount of the Moon, showing high intelligence of an imaginative order—and the Mount of Venus is almost always salient—thus giving the true poet qualities of Passion and Imagination; and these will be all the more powerful, in consequence of the absence of the restraining powers of Logic and Will.

Littered with ominous stars and crosses, this palm hints at plural wives, fatal duels – a tempestuous future indeed, 1873.

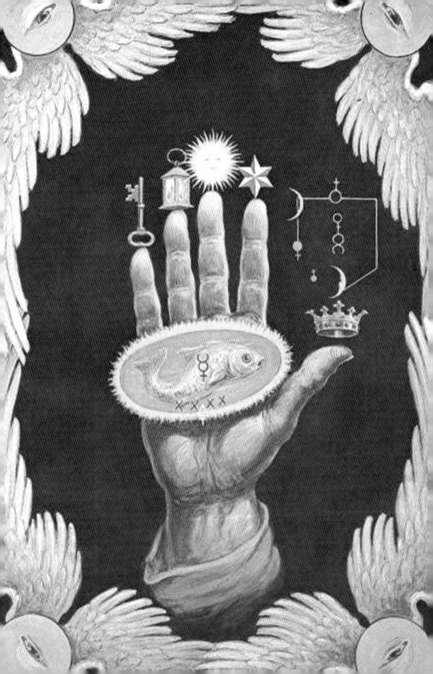

Chapter IX.

The Happy Hand.

IN conclusion we give, as our last plate on page 78, a sketch of a hand with all the lines and marks of a favourable destiny, which is called, in Palmistry, 'The Happy Hand.'

EXPLANATIONS (to correspond with plate overleaf):

a. Double Line of Life.—Perfect health and a long life.

b. The Saturnian Line, straight and well-defined.—Happiness and good fortune.

c. Branches at the end and beginning of the Line of Heart.—Excess of tenderness.

d. Cross on the Mount of Jupiter.—Love and marriage.

e. Ring of Venus.—Force of passion, but well-directed in consequence of the other good lines in the hand; in which case the Ring of Venus is not a danger, but makes the organizations richer, because fuller of capacity for pleasure.

The hand of mysteries: a lifelong obsession of Canadian mystic Manly P. Hall. According to The Secret Teachings of All Ages, *the owner of this palm has 'discovered all the treasures waiting to be found within one's own soul'.*

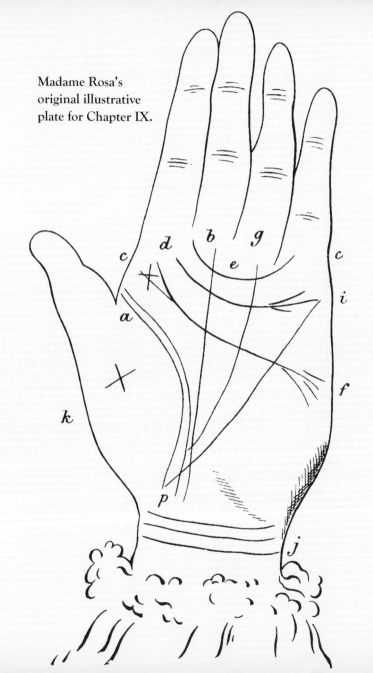

Madame Rosa's original illustrative plate for Chapter IX.

f. Genius.—The Line of Head, long, with branches at each end, and drooping towards the Mount of the Moon, which gives imagination.

g. Direct Line of Apollo.—Success in art, celebrity.

h. Union of Venus with Mercury.—Love and fortune.

i. Line of Health.—Good.

j. Triple Bracelet of the Wrist.—Superabundance of life and health.

k. Cross on the Mount of Venus.—Taken in conjunction with the same on the Mount of Jupiter, one love hallowed by marriage.

Of course, it is seldom, we may say never, that such a combination of all the gifts is to be met with on one hand; but we have seen a great many of these lines in the same hand, and in the three several instances in which we noticed this conjunction the possessors of the hands were in exceptionally happy circumstances; but such hands are rare—disappointments, anxieties, and griefs being the general rule, and happiness the exception, in this world.

The End.

All rights reserved including the right of
reproduction in whole or in part in any form
First published in 2016
by Plexus Publishing Limited
This edition copyright © 2016
by Plexus Publishing Limited
Published by Plexus Publishing Limited
The Studio, Hillgate Place
18-20 Balham Hill
London SW12 9ER
www.plexusbooks.com

British Library Cataloguing
in Publication Data
A catalogue record for this book is
available from the British Library

ISBN-13: 978-0-85965-528-6

Cover photo by Michael Steden/Shutterstock
Designed by Coco Balderrama
Printed in Europe by Imago

This book is sold subject to the condition that
it shall not by way of trade or otherwise, be
lent, re-sold, hired out or otherwise circulated
without the publisher's prior consent in any
form of binding or cover other than that in
which it is published and without a similar
condition including this condition being
imposed on the subsequent purchaser.

Acknowledgements

In the process of compiling this new
title, the editors of Plexus unearthed an
intriguing array of undeservedly forgotten
texts, illustrations and ephemera. Most
inspirational of all was Rosa Baughan's
Handbook of Palmistry. First published in 1883,
her rational approach to the ancient art of
chiromancy was decades ahead of its time.
The editors and authors are indebted to her
meticulous and illuminating research; without
her original text, this modern-day reimagining
would not have been possible. The following
sources have also been invaluable.

Books: *The Handbook of Palmistry*, Rosa
Baughan, (1883); 'A Smalle Treatise of
Palmestrie' *Summa Chiromantia*, Anon;
*Antropologium de hominis dignitate, natura et
proprietatibus, de elementis, partibus et membris
humani corporis*, Magnus Hundt, (1501); *La
Chiromancie*, Sieur de Peruchio, (1663); *The
Influence of the Stars: A Book of Old World
Lore*, Rosa Baughan, (1889); *Utriusque
Cosmi*, Robert Fludd, (1617); *De Occulta
Philosophia Libri Tres*, Heinrich Cornelius
Agrippa, (1651); *The Witches' Dream Book and
Fortune Teller*, A.H. Noe, (1874); *Manual of
Cheirosophy*, Edward Heron-Allen, (1885); *Les
mystères de la main: révélés et expliqués*, Adolphe
Desbarrolles, (1859); *Horns of Honour and
Other Studies in the By-Ways of Archaeology*,
Frederick Thomas Elworthy, (1900); *Oeuvres*,
Jean Belot, (1640); *Key to Palmistry*, Louis
Williams, (1956); *The Secret Teachings of All
Ages*, Manly Palmer Hall, (1928).

Magazines and periodicals: *Fantasio*
magazine, Vol. 3, (1917).

Websites: anamontielblog.blogspot.
co.uk, palmreadingonline.ca; nlm.nih.gov;
Gutenberg.org/ebooks; garconniere.tumblr.
com; arcive.org; etsy.com; waywardharper.
com; symbolicliving.com; openlibrary.
org; pinterest.com; books.google.com;
johnnyfincham.com; hiddenmysteries.com;
sacred-texts.com; mahalo.com;
cultofweird.com.

We would like to thank the following
for supplying photographs: Michael Steden/
Shutterstock; Charles Walker/TopFoto;
J. Balean/TopFoto; KUCO/Shutterstock;
Universal History Archive/Getty Images;
The Granger Collection/TopFoto; French
School/Getty Images; Yure/Shutterstock;
World History Archive/TopFoto;
Nadia Turner/Wayward Creations;
Chronicler/Shutterstock.

It has not always been possible to trace
copyright sources and the publisher
would be glad to hear from any such
unacknowledged copyright holders.